And Only Today

KU-373-792

To Stephen, for patience above and beyond the call of spousal duty;
to Susan Utting and Anne-Marie Fyfe for so many years of encouragement,
and to all the members of my family, still on the planet or not, for allowing me to break into their lives and steal their secrets.

Cuba in the Blood

WENDY KLEIN

WITHDRAWN FROM THE LIBRARY

KA 0374571 6

UNIVERSITY OF WINCHESTER

Published by Cinnamon Press

Meirion House, Glan yr afon, Tanygrisiau, Blaenau Ffestiniog
Gwynedd, LL41 3SU. www.cinnamonpress.com

The right of Wendy Klien to be identified as author of this work has
been asserted by her in accordance with the Copyright, Designs and
Patent Act, 1988. Copyright © 2009 Wendy Klein

ISBN: 978-1-905614-67-7

British Library Cataloguing in Publication Data. A CIP record for this
book can be obtained from the British Library.

*All rights reserved. No part of this publication may be reproduced, stored in a retrieval
system, or transmitted in any form or by any means, electronic, mechanical,
photocopying, recording or otherwise without either the prior written permission of the
publishers. This book may not be lent, hired out, resold or otherwise disposed of by way
of trade in any form of binding or cover other than that in which it is published, without
the prior consent of the publishers.*

Designed and typeset in Palatino by Cinnamon Press. Cover design by
Mike Fortune-Wood from original artwork 'Havana facade and
oldtimer' by Roxane Gonzalez, agency: dreamstime.com.

Printed by the MPG Books Group in the UK

Acknowledgments

Many thanks to the editors of publications in which some of these
poems have appeared previously: *Magma, Smith's Knoll, Envoi, Poetry
Nottingham*, and to the Ware, Ver and Pitshanger Poets, whose
competition anthologies have found places for other poems in this
collection. Thanks are due as well to the hard-core members (you know
who you are) of the Reading Thin Raft Poetry group, who have helped
me to beat many of these poems into more acceptable shape and to
Ashley Harrold (afh), the witty compere at Reading Poets' Cafe, who
makes a fantastic contribution to keeping poetry vibrant in Reading and
even lets me read more than one poem sometimes. Additional thanks to
the poet, Peter Carpenter whose contagious enthusiasm kick-started
some of the more recent poems published here, the poet Jane Draycott,
whose River and Rowing Museum workshops have been a marvellous
source of inspiration over time and to the New Orleans poet, Jan
Villarrubia, who has buoyed me up at so many stages during the fine-
tuning of the final manuscript. Last but not least, heartfelt thanks to
Cinnamon editor, Jan Fortune-Wood, who had sufficient faith to mount
the project and who has remained positive and supportive throughout.

Contents

UNIVERSITY OF WINCHESTER
LIBRARY

Cuba Notebook:

UNIVERSITY OF WINCHESTER	
03745716	821.92 WE

Stops Along the Fault-line:

Cuba in the Blood

Cuba Notebook

i. *My First Cuba*
my grandfather in 1899

I sit on his lap, my throne
as he shows me the photos
he keeps in a cardboard box
covered with stains, with squiggly
letters in an unfamiliar alphabet.

The box is full of pictures
of dead people, and
if they're not put in right
the lid won't shut. Today
he shows me a shot in sepia;
a young man I don't know.

From my lap-throne I trace
the scar on his forehead, made
by a rock thrown by a Cossack
during a pogrom. Pogroms
are yesterday's history; today's
is different. I prepare myself.

The man in the photo wears
a wide-brimmed hat, even then
he wore a hat—my dashing grandpa—
his face stern with responsibility
for saving Cuba from Spain;
my grandpa, the brave soldier.

High on a horse he takes command
of the island, the world, my heart;
serves the country that saved him
from Cossacks; sent him to occupy
the home of coconut palms, turquoise
water, bronzed faces. Decades pass.
Now I touch the medals he's earned

from the government of America
by not breaking sweat with Teddy's
Rough Riders, but sitting proud
in the saddle in front of his barracks,
and already I ache for that island:

the sting of lime, the scorch of rum.
My feet begin to twitch and tingle
to a beat I can only imagine, my hips
sway to rhythms I've yet to hear;
vistas only guessed at: my next Cuba.

*In the airport departure lounge I'm thinking about my father;
how he prefaced every journey with, 'travel is travail' as he
checked and re-checked the many lists that increased with his
galloping dementia.*

ii. Flight Pattern

What if I walked; what if
I just walked away—now?

What if I just walked
past that cleaner swathed

in modest dress, her scarlet uniform
aching with morning. What if

I ignored the tug of my own dress
skinny, black, hobbling my ankles?

What if I just stepped over the feet of that
African man clutching plastic bags

of duty frees to his broad batik chest,
past the synthetic curls of the perfumed

counter staff, their waterproof mascara
getting ready to resist tears all day,

slipped behind the racks of sunglasses that
turn to follow me, past duty free cigarettes,

reminding me I've stopped, but the craving
has not. Then what if I sauntered right past security

walking the wrong way? Even a terrorist
might be invisible, walking the wrong way.

Picking up speed through passport control
skipping along the pavement outside,

breathing-in diesel fuel and freedom, I could
disappear seamlessly, into the patchwork crowd.

iii. Flight

In the high thin air above Madrid
the sun sets in fiery haste, leaves
a wonderful starry-straight track
like a pheasant's footsteps jotted
across clouds, and the bar is open
all night to fellow travellers who
go there for different reasons...

iv. Fellow Traveller

He tells you he's a farmer—going
for the bonefishing—been tying
flies each night for months,
excited by the stalking,
the sight-casting,
the adrenaline rush.

You picture him,
lips taut with effort, pinching up
the bright feathers, the line—
transparent, trailing across his palms,
the cool lead of the weights; the knots,
snug, satisfying.

From a boat, you ask? And he talks
about the flat water—standing in it
thigh-deep, squinting into the Cuban sun,
picking out each staccato jerk of the
lure—the hunter and his quarry: exhausted,
caught, then released
unharmed.

You think of Hemingway,
twist your hands to stop yourself
reaching out to touch his ponytail—
airbrushed grey, saucy—and his cheek,
furred with incipient beard, hands
thick-fingered with milking cows,
delivering lambs, totting up profits,
pausing over losses,

and you shiver when you think
of the might-be nights
that would smell of fish and soap,
taste of salt, and the moment
you would both let your hair down;
of his beard when it's full and soft;
of the day when it's time to go home
to your knotting and tying.

v. Landing con Amigos

We hardly know them—
        blizzards of emails over four years—
                a snowfall of warmth,
but they are there
        with *besos*, not the thin air
                kisses of France,
but the fleshly kisses
        of Cuba. Their colours—
                utter blackness and whiteness dazzle—
between them Cuba's skin of contrasts,
        and we are
                cosseted; guided—taxis, lights, love.

vi. Late Arrival in Havana Vieja

Night: shuffle, bump of luggage and we drop
on the old town *Havana vieja* honoured guests,
offered, like Hemingway, the first Mojitas,

their lime bite, crunch of undissolved sugar, wallop
of unmeasured rum. Later, ensconced in the bridal suite—
the irony—there is foreign cheese, and wine—soft, red, French.

The globe of evening hangs over us, and we drink
in exhaustion, drink to our success; to making it here
for the second time, drink until the bottle stands empty.

Things that are clear in a drunken moment, may not hold
water elsewhere. There is no hot water to wash; the smell
of medieval, moist and timeless as stone, as musk, drips.

vii. First Day—From the Balcony

The shutters protest my prod and push, quake
and groan at my clumsiness, shed dust, flakes
of paint that curl and crumble between fingers.

I stand back, shelter in the dusk of a room
that will hold its dark and cool all day, hope
no one can see me in my nightdress, too white

and frilly against the glare of the tropical sun,
but no one is looking in this morning's Havana.
Out there, as remembered, the retinal overload

of rooftops red-tiled, houses hand-painted
in the pinks and greens of sherbet, like
the souvenir bowls sold in every shop.

A woman, two floors up, lowers a basket
on a rope so long it reaches the bread seller
two floors down, turns, bangs her door

on laundry that might be rags elsewhere,
hangs in elegant tatters here. Next-door
to her a Dachshund—stocky, outraged,

shut out on its balcony—wails at its owners,
who must be deaf or indifferent,
at passers-by, at me, fizzing, buzzing

as I anticipate the first beat of a street band,
the muted *por favor* of beggars, the silent
pleas of street dogs—always hungry,

rarely fed—poignant in their politeness;
the undercurrent of little deaths in back
rooms. Lorries belch black plumes

of bad fuel like indignant farts that thin
to sludge-grey, disappear into a sky
already smogged. The street waits.

viii. A Parrot Comes to Breakfast

Patio open to the sky; a smother of ferns,
of orchids, coleus, tropical palms, and a parrot,
unfettered, uncaged, uses his beak to assist

his climb up my chair-leg to the summit
of the table, his goal dry bread, black coffee.
Wise-eyed over his crampon hooks he makes

eye-contact, senses capitulation, shakes
his feather-mantel, scatters shreds of emerald;
preens his breast, sheds ruby splinters.

Sociable, calm, shrewd, he flaps up the stairwell,
leans over the banister, and with a single triumphant
squawk, takes charge. Meanwhile the chef

fries onions for lunch, for a dish that will never taste
as good as it smells; outside the ubiquitous
stink of imperfect drains greets the morning.

ix. Afternoon and Rain

Havana harbour — the bay full — a load
of dumped pineapples like disembodied
heads. Plastic bottles are dead gulls,

as, footsore, glutted with sensation, weighed
down with everything deep-fried in batter,
we sit on the harbour wall. The sun has tried

and failed to come out, greying nets whoosh,
billow, unfurl like dirty flags from windows
of high-rise flats, street-wise dogs, seek shelter.

Rain, unexpected in Havana, the anonymity of it,
the way it turns the greys to black, fades everywhere
it lands; widens the cracks the sun's picked out.

We take cover in a café, drink coffee, track the wind's
erratic path, the way it blows everything dry so fast
the wet is forgotten; we head back to the hotel.

x. Generic

He may be some shade of brown,
indeterminate, but in the range
from beige to burnt sienna.

She may be low-slung, but alert
and unruffled, with dangling dugs,
left over from her last litter.

He may be 100% male, proud
of his *cojones*; wearing them
bulging and visible from every angle.

Whatever the gender, it's a mistake
to underestimate the generic brown
dog of Havana. This dog knows its way

through the barrios; dodges taxis
and Caddies with tail-fins to die for—
or under. This dog is purposeful—

at all times, ferreting out the scarce shade,
occupying it under the benevolent
stone gaze of revolutionary heroes: José Martí,

Che Guevara, of Fidel himself, while
wringing the hearts, over and over,
of the generic capitalist tourist.

xi. Beat

Backstreets like bombsites,
their buzz of renovation,

revolution. I walk fast, eyes fixed
on the cobbles, avoiding

cavernous gaps. From somewhere,
a beat: persistent, seductive,

African, stops me. I expect kids
with attitude, hip-swivelling

past, or the rumba dancers who get paid
to fake ethnic for tourists; parade

metres high on stilts, but from behind me,
in a coverall, a woman beats

immaculate salsa, her water bottle,
jungle-hollow, thwacks her thigh: boom,

boom—tack, tack, someone's grandmother,
hair twisted in short grey dreads—dadada,

pause, dah, the way she steps dance-time,
beams toothless joy.

*Siesta time, with an evening of Salsa looming; a tropical night
in the city…*

xii. Havana

She's an old whore who drags
her soiled petticoats,
through the moist dark.

The leather seats of her taxis are cracked
by old trysts, the fenders dented
by bodies from another time.

She side-steps around young girls
in stilettos, out late looking for work
finding it, their tawny legs

insinuated between
the thighs of men who were
weary just minutes ago,

but no longer, as their flies are
fingered, their grizzled pates stroked by
warm hands, their backs pressed tight

against rusty wrought-iron gates,
leaving a filigree imprint that
will remind them tomorrow

of rumba in Havana.
The red light of her cigarillo moves,
and with each inhalation,

flashes a tight Morse code: the sting
of the smoke, the flare of her nostrils,
more sensed than seen. She's a lady dragon

and she'll take them inside her hot tunnel mouth,
sear their flesh with her cinnamon tongue,
musky and wise with nicotine;

brown with the last smoke of evening,
before lying down, and the first smoke of morning,
before lying down again.

Smoke, she hums, gets in your eyes, and
sly as the rising breeze brushing bare flesh,
the palm leaves will croon the chorus.

xiii. Two Days in — Pinar del Rio

Driving inland to Viñales Valley and Pinar del Rio National Park, you share the Cuban national highway—wide, unmarked—with American cars from the 50s, held together with paste and plastic, maintained with screw drivers, endless fiddling and love. You overtake horse-drawn carts, whole families balanced on one listing bicycle, open lorries, jam-packed with workers who overflow their sides in faded denim, straw hats, a refrigerator being hauled in for service on a cart powered by a pair of oxen. Everywhere hitchhikers implore you with their arms, their eyes, offer fistfuls of money, stampede towards you if you dare to slow down. A hen, intrepid with stupidity, leads her young family, balls of fluff, ridiculous on toothpick legs, into the fast lane, changes her mind, retreats. Miraculously no one is crushed as brakes squeal—here, at least, life is not, not ever, cheap.

Off the main road are pot-holes like canyons. You lurch through villages, past houses with unglazed windows, barefoot children, the distance defined by slender palms that jut into the sky; a drive-through museum of Cuban art— Garcia, Enriquez, Landaluze, Abela—through paintings, posters, travel brochures that do not once lie about the exotic beauty of this place. Viñales National Park was created as a biosphere in the 1960s, and in line with its ethos, the Hotel Moka shares its space with the tree that was there first and now spreads through the roof of the reception area, stretches to a cloud-scudded sky.

xiv. Day Three— The Biosphere, a Canopy of Contradictions

light so faint
my eyelids resist
the signal to open
oppressed by the weight
of impending rain
that squeezes my sinuses
already swollen
I am braced
for its crescendo
awake to an undertow
of homesickness
that threatens
to drown me
a lump in my gut

where the food of equality
rice and beans
has become my food of affliction
in this Cuban Exodus
where I rise
to the challenge
of the next excursion

A Walk in the Biosphere

He has the green-sea eyes, fair colouring of the un-evolved Cuban, our guide, in contrast to the mottled skins, missing teeth of the cabin people who live on the edge of the park, and we ask about their abject poverty, the tumble of dirty children, emaciated bitches hounded by starving puppies. He frowns, launches into rhetoric, a seduction of facts: how it was worse than it was before; how the project began; how, in the 1960s, the government asked for volunteers to leave their homes behind to create the communal idyll where animals, plants and people would live together in harmony and cooperation, in the new not-abject poverty; how he has lived here all his life, his classmates still his best friends, and we try to imagine growing up in a biosphere, everything feeding back into everything else—your 27 classmates part of it— where everyone will eat; will volunteer to eat, rice and beans; will shut their doors on the places they were born, to chase the ideal of a shared agriculture in the ruins of 'El Contento' a coffee plantation once worked by slaves, owned, he says with a white smile of triumph, by an Englishman.

El Contento rears up in a twist of vines that give way to crumbling stone walls that drop debris in chunks, in flakes, and everywhere Bursera Simaruba, the tourist tree, its bark peeling, exposing red flesh...

xv. Gumbo Limbo

West Indian birch tree,
spread he skinny arms,

reach for sky
bark peel - red

like tourist;
tolerate most wind

even hurricane—
bark make better:

poison ivy
kill bacteria

take away pain
take way fever

stop bleeding
make more peepee

more sex
tourist see

how sexy
is Cuba.

Viñales

Not much more than village, it boasts the best cigar brands in
Cuba. Legend has it that the plant grows even better if you
speak to it; that the best cigars are rolled on the thighs of
virgins. Although cigars are still entirely made by hand here,
a visit to a factory tells another story.

xvi. Cigar Factory

Everywhere the brown rustle of the leaves
where it is sorted, stacked and rolled by row

on row of bored women, against the drone
of live readings—twice a day for half an hour:

the newspaper, poetry, a chapter from a novel.
They race nimble-fingered, vie with one another

for bonuses, laugh, gossip and like the caterpillars
that live off the leaves of the growing plant,

take on the aroma of tobacco before devouring it;
the workers focus blindly; don't spare a glance

at the wallpaper of political slogans, hand-
lettered: *Viva la revolución, Socialism o muerte,*

Hasta la victoria siempre… Impossible to pick out
the virgins, all thighs tucked demurely under

their tables. Everywhere dim, the light kept low,
so the leaf, bright green like a child to start,

ripened now to deep toasted brown to be inhaled,
chewed or burnt, becomes like time itself,

ends up in old age as wisps of smoke.

UNIVERSITY OF WINCHESTER
LIBRARY

Las Jazmines Hotel

We arrive after lunch, and the sky spends the afternoon filling up with trouble, makes us stick to our claustrophobic cabin; start a desultory game of Scrabble...

xvii. Tropical Storm

Thick yellow air, the consistency of soup;
our room, a tight box in a row of others,
close, grey;
a patio the only place to breathe.

The wind is up, the sky malicious.
A small dog, black and white brow furrowed,
arrives, begs, but not for food,
takes refuge under my chair
as thunder
growls up the valley,
followed by lightning
so close
there's no gap between sound and flash.

Rain batters the pavement, splashes my feet
so I fold my chair away.
My dog, deprived of shelter, reverts
so fast
to instinct
I gasp as he digs, red earth flying,
digs up the flower box
that separates our unit from our neighbour's,
digs himself a hole the exact size of his body,
huddles in it,
eyes tight shut—

is still there when I open the door to morning.

xviii. Dawn

drum of rain ceased
in front of every cabin
awed figures in a silence
scored with camera clicks
attempt to capture
a medieval landscape
a Brueghel tableau
tucked in the corners
of the canvas lovers
who embrace oblivious
to the carnage around them
where as the checkerboard
life below crowns
through creation-mist
layered in sheets
where limestone mountains
nudge their Jurassic heads
like drowsy dinosaurs
a landscape so primitive
you expect Tyrannosaurus
to stretch out his jointed limbs
towards a pinkening west
the creak of time the leathery
flap of Pterodactyl wings
and a buzzard
that might be Pterosaurus
contemplates a white horse
its rider ungendered
by distance
followed by a black dog
running hard
and we are awake
to the affection of hungry dogs
a mule on a hill
tethered just out of reach
of grass

a waterfall of green
the plague of mimosa
a lizard-eye view of life
above below
greedy to take part

El Palenque

*We thread our way through yesterday's prehistoric terrain,
last night's storm already burnt away by late morning sun, a
thread of wispy clouds its sole reminder, towards El
Palenque, one of the places, says the guide book, where
runaway slaves could escape from their masters prior to the
abolition of slavery in Cuba. Ahead a tiny sign and what
looks like the open jaws of a massive shark—the entrance to a
cave and through it a bar and restaurant with tables, chairs,
loudspeaker system, stage carved out of stone, an
advertisement for the upcoming appearance of Los Zafiros, a
Cuban pop group, coming this Saturday night; everything
noisy with the colours of Santeria, the religious fusion
between Christianity and ancient African beliefs, and our
guide points out a young woman dressed in white.*

xvix. Day Job

Out of the shark's mouth *Palenque* you glide,
white-turbaned head a beacon of dignity; turn
your back on the cave, the camp, the fake fire,

its glow, electric orange. On you, the shapeless slave
shift is a Dior gown bleached with sun-power
that brings out the dark sheen of your skin, the colour

of your grandmothers who escaped the night-time
visits. You're dressed up for your job as a *Cimarron*,
a runaway slave; which you do each day with a certain

sullen pride, strict about your breaks for tobacco;
for coffee. I watch you saunter back to the cave through
the restaurant, pack of smokes in hand, leave its Santeria

splendour, wonder if you sacrifice to these African gods:
Obatala, the purest, owner of everything white, snow,
clouds, silver, bones, brain; Yemaya, lady of the sea

and moon, the mother wrapped in the virgin blue of your
catechism. Or perhaps you pray to Oya, generous but implacable;
lady of wind, fire, and thunder, who dances violently, waves

a horse tail; or if it is her little sister Ochun, lady of love, sexuality
who glows sun-yellow, queens rivers, who is your inspiration?
Our guide laughs, swipes at your arse as you leave—says, she doesn't

like me, but she really loves me. He is white as your black is black,
the white of the night-time visitors who planted their pallid seed;
made Cuba blossom all the mulatto shades of *café con leche*.

xx. Back to Havana

*In a taxi, hurtling from the vulgarity that is Jibacoa, past oil pumps,
14 kilometres of beach, and the smell of the fresh pumpings—
childhood memories of California, the Joshua trees on the hill holding
up their crooked arms to the undecided sky, the sea, its violent
Southern blues and greens—I ponder how we have managed in the
face of unnatural beauty and tantalising contradictions, what Che
Guevara would have made of it all…*

xxi. Jibacoa—a Peaceful Retirement for Che

A swathe of gulls, their anger wakes him
and under his pillow: *nada.* Ayee

that chambermaid has moved his *pistoles*—
unloaded for now. *Pero sus ojos verdes,*

but her green eyes, like seas, or ice water, the way
her visits transform his room, towels

twisted into swans, their necks in amorous coils,
sangria hibiscus tucked in the creases.

Oof, how the room is over-heated, over-sexed
by her scent: sweat and disinfectant,

but *si,* revolutionary spirit. She has removed
those signs that say, in six languages—no smoking,

laid out his cigars next to an ashtray big enough
for a *comandante,* or a tourist.

Through the slit-blind shutters, he can see spiky
bromeliads strapped to banana palms, sand;

a landscape that makes no sense—no camouflage
for his guerrillas where the sun picks out

snake-arm chairs made of dyed bamboo. He shuts
his eyes on missed Bolivia, reflects

on revolutions that end in bad roads, food rations,
wonders about the wind's invitation—

a day out fishing for marlin, with Fidel
or that other Ernesto.

Penultimate day –
Hemingway Museum Finca Vigia (Lookout Farm)

Another taxi; smog, traffic, sprawl of suburbs en route to San Francisco de Paula, the Hemingway museum, newly reopened, and we're met by a guide who tells us with such pride, how much 'Papa' was loved and revered by Cubans, especially the poor fisherman, their families—an outpouring of official tenderness—where Pilar, the boat he fished from, stands in dry-dock, endures restoration; room after room of the mansion roped off, 6,000 books their covers fading, the walls festooned with dead animals; proof of his virility; concrete, conclusive. How facts and legends intertwine; Ketchum Idaho, on weekend leave from a psychiatric hospital, depressed after intensive ECT, alarmed at subsequent memory loss, he picked up his gun for the last time; turned it on himself; how Mary, his last wife, distraught, told the press he was just cleaning the weapon…

xxii. Papa

Not the tower that Mary, his fourth,
had built to contain
his feral genius,

but where he shut his six-toed cats
inside at night; instructed
his protégée, Italian,

adoring, seventeen. Nor the pool where
he watched Ava Gardner swim
naked—told men

as they dipped, what the water had seen,
touched, and was entertained
by their response.

31

Not even his weight-charts that never varied
much, pencilled in each day on the wall
above the scales,

or his favourite chair, or that lizard preserved
in formaldehyde, who fought off cats—
died well. Certainly not

the bodiless trophies of dead beasts, their glassy
gaze that dominates every room,
their sleek pelts

stretched out under his horny feet; mighty hunter—
old jade. None of these, but the typewriter,
a portable Royal,

placed waist-high on a bookcase in the yellow-
tiled room, where he stood each day
to write, let his legs

tell him when it was time to stop. I would knock
down the tower, drown the pool in earth,
plant over it with fragrant

shrubs and trees—jasmine, magnolia, jacaranda;
cremate what is left of the beasts,
but that squat twin

to my mother's battered machine, that I would keep;
place it high enough to remind me
when to stop.

Last day

At a loose-end, packing done, we wander into an overcast afternoon, find the National Museum of Cuban Art, stray from the marked route, are sanctioned by the uniformed guards who stand in cross-armed authority in every dim-lit room, discover some Cuban differences…

xxiii. National Museum, Havana— El Rapto de las Mulatas, Carlos Enriquez

About Enriquez, he did not pretend. Cuban
to the core, he painted peasants, bandits,
sensual women, restless horses against

a backdrop of palm trees, rolling hills. Trained
accountant, self-taught painter, his life was
drunken, erratic, short—wild as this painting.

It takes a moment to work out this is rape,
the Sabine women transferred to Cuban fields.
The palm trees lean back in alarm, fronds

like the frantic hands of the woman on her back,
braced against the horse, its neck arched in its own
protest. Her fingers flare, while her garments spread

around her in sunset shades, a tangle of legs. The hats
of the *bandoleros*, their ammunition belted across
their chests and shoulders, are pulled low, obscure

their faces except for lips—a smile that might be lewd,
a moustache pencilled in, brown hands neither gentle
nor cruel. This ferocity that could be rape or rapture

raises questions about the artist; the nature of the act.
Enriquez had a horse brought to his workshop; tied
the female model to its back; had it lashed to create

a more realistic scene. The women, after his favourite
model, Sara Cheméndez, are painted as fusion between
rapture and rape: the sky both turbulent and soft at once,

its pinks and mauves too harsh to be ambivalence,
too lush to be surrender.

*So much of Cuba is like returning to the 'fifties, my time, but
never is that clearer than on the last evening when I see a car,
a 1952 Chevrolet, the twin of the one that taught me to drive.*

xxiv. Still Life with Car

It might have been mine,
nightmared straight from my adolescence
to a field near a caravan, tyres missing
like limbs lopped off, grill, gap-toothed,
grinning, a Chevy cross, its red badge of courage.

Or it might have been my father's, when fins first
arrived, grew to grotesque proportions, the metal
burgeoning blue as Bermuda sharks—the car
she threatened to leap from driving home
from the coast, where she'd confronted him
about his latest infidelity.

But maybe it was just itself, harbouring
its own secrets about who had sex
with who in the back seat, and when—
got pregnant, ran off after—
and who crumpled the bumper first.

34

Leave-taking —
xxv. My Last Cuba

You are, I think, asleep, but your presence fills
the cavern of this room, the bridal suite

where we started ten days ago. The bloodshot
eye of the smoke detector winks

at tower height above the mysterious platform
we took to be a minstrel gallery.

Your easy breath keeps me anchored, the way
it is punctuated with snores

and sniffs, comes and goes less smoothly as you
ease yourself into morning, and

I unwrap the plate we bought together; shapes
that will tell us where we were yesterday,

will remind us down the line where we were today:
the primary colours; the primitive forms;

remind us the laundry that danced on the balcony
opposite was only rags

made elegant through time's wrought-iron
rusting filter.

Stops Along the Fault-line

How, Honourable to the Letter, He Keeps his Promise to his Granddaughter Despite Inauspicious Circumstances

The morning's earthquake-breath does not deter him;
the heave and sway of the shower tiles under his feet
like a Disney floor, the wave of nausea that follows
each tremor, the soar up the Richter scale. The trip

will go ahead as planned. I see him, feet bunioned into
brogues, tie throttled with a Windsor knot, hat, a Panama
jammed on his head, the way he licks his lips, hypertensive
purple, yanks the choke to full, posts on the accelerator.

His Pontiac, serious in grey, stays cool across the Mojave, though
its bonnet dazzles from excessive buffing. He waltzes it round
the Tehachapi Loop, down through the valley towards Bakersfield;
follows the fault-line to wherever I am waiting.

The Letters Between Us

for Samuel Heyert (1879 – 1962)

How he yearned to teach me the alphabets that shaped him,
landed him between the Byzantine curls of Cyrillic,
its traps and surprises: the A, M, and T,
so like English, the hooded back-to-front 'b',
a footstool beneath its seraphed canopy
and the sternness of prayer book Hebrew.

From his *Siddur,* he would trace squat *Chet,*
the inquisitive curve of *Lamed,* severe *Dalet,*
using his forefinger as *yod,* read backwards across the page,
tap each word, speak it, lingering over the ghetto gutturals
as he tried and failed to climb out of his past:
the shtetl, the steerage, the black-gabardine chanting.

And I was a dull pupil, reproached in the letters
he fired at me through all my growing away,
envelopes addressed in poles and pikes:
i's dotted with emphatic bursts, strident t's,
the twin-spiked 'W' of my name, the Y's tail so straight
its spine must have ached from the jab of his Parker 51.

It was grandmother's postscripts:
the clean curves of the fifth-grade school-leaver,
her model penmanship, that soothed me, delivered
her smells to me off the page—a blend of mothballs
and face powder; the comfort of misspellings
and devotion.

What would they think of this draughtsman's pencil,
my sturdy blue life-line, its clumsiness, its smudges; my hope
that something fresh will emerge; can be rubbed out if not;
the way I shape my letters, sloped back with resistance,
rearward-leaning, forward-lurching—left-handed writing
in a right-handed person?

How, snagged in the Velcro of memory,
it becomes more illegible, how I use it to conjure him,
wonder if what I'd read as pedantry, was only pastiche—
the reproach, a wildcard love—
whether we ever climb out of our pasts:
the shtetl, the steerage, the black-gabardine chanting.

Loose Stones

I used to believe
that tigers didn't matter, unless
you were a native child
about to be devoured.

I thought
if I didn't hold my breath, cross my fingers double,
the plane would plummet
in flames and screams;

that though he wore
pin stripes, a mafia hat, my grandfather
was surely Abraham. I could see
the knife, hear the ram protest.

He was not,
but when I catch the eye of certain
men, I feel the need to cover my throat.

I always knew
that lying should be used only
in emergencies—not to rely on special effects.

More recently, I'd put my faith
in laundry, its friendly weight, wet or dry,
breathing in wholesome, the bulk of it filling
up memory.

Only now, as suddenly,
tapping loose stones, their descent, suicidal,
down vertical slopes, their bodies, arcs of white, gold
and grey, recalling the bull dancers of Crete,

stopping to graze on the
sleeping volcano that is Santorini,
have I realised the integrity of goats—the occasion
of the unrehearsed moment—
its absolute purity.

Percale

Still in wrappers, stiff
with cardboard, the sheen
of cellophane; every visit
percale sheets—white.
to match my pinched face.

How they felt like satin,
crackled when she shook them,
spread them out for me to touch
with washed hands,
with reverence. How

they hurt like snow
brought tears, an ache
of cold on bony feet,
sliding into bed—
like skinned sardines.

Preserved

Moonlit tombstone white,
neon flicker blue, it wobbled
and shuddered in turn.

Or it hummed, gargantuan and comforting,
while resident vegetables broke out in new life,
developed antibiotic propensities;

where a chicken leg lay, half-naked
in a scrap of tin foil, behind a tower of dried
broad beans, mysterious in their torn packet;

where cheese might embark, smelly-footed, on journeys
of its own, to orgiastic unions with fermenting fruit
in that holy grail: my grandmother's Frigidaire.

Each day, in a ritual to appease the gods of waste,
she emptied it onto the table, mumbling a prayer
that some hero, ravenous and greedy,

would wolf down the lot, finish it off,
along with the murky scrap of Borscht,
that lurked, unnaturally purple.

Like her recurrent dream
of fleeing through the streets
in her night dress,

a city behind her in flames,
the phantoms of need
ganged up on her —

assaulted her — near the end,
nipping
at her bare heels.

Bridging

The bridge stretches out toward sunrise;
its orange, that masquerades as gold,
takes me from goodbye to goodbye,

reminds me how every journey starts in tears,
ends in tears, and I am back just outside
Flagstaff, lightning jagging the dark, the thunk

under the wheels the year my father killed
the Easter bunny, and I wailed without a break
to Phoenix, Tucson, the Mexican border;

which takes me to another drive, home again from
the coast, when mother had learned of his latest
woman—tried to jump out on the freeway; how he

stopped in time, and me wondering what if he had not;
seeing us limp along together; the wait for the next one—
would I like her? Sun full in my face, I remember

when he ceased to be able to cross bridges; when
his suspension failed him once-and-for-all
as we drove across to see Lucia da Lammermoor,

broke down on Van Ness Avenue, missed it; how
no perfect journey involves a car unless it is driven
by Bud on a Sunday afternoon in Utah, the red, red

rock face of the canyons from his flat-mate's clapped out
MG, green, unheated; the concert later, the candle
at the foot of the bed before I found out about his fiancée

in New York; the goodbye-morning. A plane takes off
close by, shadows the bonnet of this rental car,
its compact neutrality. Like a silver toy,

it gets smaller and smaller as it climbs, disappears
behind clouds, offers journeys that might end
in tears or might end somewhere else.

Kid Gloves

Put up your dukes he chortles   fists
clenched feinting

Dad's happy again got a new job
keep moving he yells

Watch your feet Sugar Ray would win
by dancing

You know I was semi-pro once he tells her
on a tramp steamer   sailed

the world   He was good kept his guard
up tells her to do the same

Now she's bunched up   wards off blows,
hears herself shriek   wonders

why he doesn't see her tears but thinks
it beats the tickling

when she's fending off his fingers when
the gloves are off

Slipping out Early

My father's collecting beer cans again;
his latest mission. He's slipped out early
in his Giants baseball cap; his sweater
buttoned up all wrong; the hem unravelled.
Mother hasn't noticed, might not find out
until he's brought back by a policeman,
grinning, a close call. He's forgotten he was

an English teacher, born, he used to say, with
a silver spoon in his mouth. At the supermarket
they give him five cents a can, and he thinks
he's amassing a fortune against the next depression—
no more blue-plate specials—just *à la carte*. Once
he sent a kid into the marshes to fetch a can he couldn't
reach; risked drowning him, another close call.

Last night's television was full of wild animals;
big cats that killed elephants, the camera crew excited,
but distressed, though they seemed to know a bit about
nature, about narrow escapes, dangerous shots. It made me
think of him: his wildcat enthusiasms, the tug of his last
mission, his close calls; how little I knew him,
how much I am like him.

UNIVERSITY OF WINCHESTER
LIBRARY

Songs my Stepmother Taught me

It's your face embossed on the harvest moon
every birthday; the camel beige of suntans nurtured
with baby oil and beer, followed by martinis at five.

There was you in charge at the piano, shuffling dreams like
well-thumbed sheet music—*where the deep purple falls*
over sleepy garden walls. Your voice picked up volume
while your fingers picked out chords, not with the graceless
fumbling of your mothering, but gathering them into
submission with gentle respect; a courtship without force
in an old fashioned garden. All the dip and swish
of modesty filled the evening; shy girls in dirndl skirts,
hesitant kisses, hot with expectation, dry with inexperience,
and boys from the nearby airbase in uniform; in their cups.

There was I, hitting all the high notes, your contralto laying
down the harmony, grounding my girlish soprano—weak,
with a tendency towards flatness. It was months before you'd
find me in his sleeping bag, old testament rain drilling the tent;
drag me out with threats and prophecies; send him packing
with tears and tea, with *shine on, shine on harvest moon.*

Dismantling her Bed

for Hannah

Her skill with an Allen key unlocks it
and baseboards loosen
clatter like marionettes set free;

a marimba keyboard strapped together
with strips of grosgrain ribbon
that look too weak to have kept her safe

during all her growing-up in the attic room
above our heads, each plank
a gossip of history,

the bounce and spring of her body
at rest and at play, a tittle-tattle
that told the first thump of morning

the footsteps that creaked reassurance.
Shouldn't we wait for your dad, I say
but her brisk, *sisters are doing it*

themselves these days reminds me
the van is waiting. She shrouds
me in scarves gifted birthdays ago,

and I plant out wallflowers
for my spring garden, pot-up herbs
for her first balcony.

Three-dog Night

for Robin

Because I was poor
and you were portable
I took you with me
everywhere. There was

no Moses basket, only pools
of coats, quilted, embroidered,
of shawls, soft or scratchy—
makeshift beds in hippy houses

all over the world. In your
blanket sleeper, your eyes
closing already, anticipating
the soporific stuff of coats,

we lay down together on floors
on landings, on strange beds—
wherever the coats of guests
were left. Sometimes I told you

the story of the Aborigine boy, how
he slept curled round his dog
for warmth, and as the nights grew
colder, invited a second, then

the coldest: three-dog night.
By the third dog you were asleep—
always. I could slip out, door
ajar in case you stirred, leave

you to breathe in, second-hand,
cannabis, patchouli joss sticks, cheap
red wine, to learn to share your bed
with furtive lovers, family pets,

weeping drunks of both sexes—
a comprehensive education of life.
Very soon you got the hang
of covering yourself with coats—

in railway stations, on freezing trains
on late-night couches—became proud
of my gift to you: the ability
to make your bed almost anywhere.

Just North of April

how just outside Newcastle
you've scandalised that couple
across the aisle
with your plastic cups of wine

and the doomed lambs
are beginning to pall
no messages on your mobile
you've left your water bottle

behind on the table
your one true source of sustenance
in the desert of travel
and you wish

you could have left a pie
the crust gold
crisped with butter
the filling her favourite fruit

succulent but not too sweet
placed it on the tile
you once brought her from Turkey
a gazelle glazed in turquoise

the tender glance of its one-way eye
or a box of perfect chocolates
expensive enough to be important
but time runs out

during post-breakfast philosophy
Plato Schopenhauer
drowned out by the wails
of squabbling children

you are left with unfinished phrases
the alarm of the eight-year-old
who heard cemetery for symmetry
after the thrust and grunt

of an afternoon moving furniture
the afterglow of hope
some faint genetic imprint
our particular symmetry

Some Midnights

I am from nowhere in particular
nowhere that's on any map
but I go back at certain times
red and blue moons
the winter solstice
some midnights
search for clues in box
after box of torn photographs
tarnished costume jewellery
look for your face in shots
of high-breasted women
uncorseted competent
who smile mysteriously
from under big hats
their hands always folded
hands not unlike my own
that can bake stitch
hold a pencil in private
make it speak for them

and in the crackling air
before the hem of sleep
comes unstitched
I expect you any minute
to step through the arch
of my longing
in a Chanel suit
or a Dior gown

your wrists heavy with bracelets
not unlike the ones
in those boxes
your lips paint-box vermillion
I wait for you to lean down
tattoo my cheek
with their colour whisper
what comes next
when I don't know

What my Mother had in Common with Murillo

…his self-portrait—painted to portray himself for the wishes and prayers of his children…

The pose, every movement staged,
and lace trim at the neck; his hand
that reaches out from inside the mirror,
rests on the frame, sure of its place
in the composition, the extinction
of the everyday, the utter presence.
But here the commonality falters—
except for his palette, everything
applied without colour—while she,
the queen of unsolved mysteries,
painted her life in pink, in orange,
I imagine her smoking a cigarette
in front of a mirror in the dark—
the movement to and from her lips,
like the fireflies that Long Island
summer, catching them in jars,
their torpedo bodies: the smell of smoke—
antique mirrors—
more ghost than smile.

Caught Between a Hurricane and What-Happens-Next; her Life in Miniature

She is born in the Bronx: pink, blonde, cute. It is
not enough; no plastic ballerina twirling on a single
screw in a tutu made of cheesecloth, or some sorry
excuse for the kind of net that could catch anything
and keep it, and keep it. Pearl Harbour is bombed,
hysteria reigns; it will stay like that. She grows up
too fast, pairs up too young—falls open like a jewellery
box—everything sparkly: Golden Gate baby, red dress
in Macy's, the President shot dead in Dallas. Hysteria
reigns; it will stay like that. She flies away to Europe,
a balsa wood pilot in love with flight: splits up, pairs up,
moves on, splits up, pairs up again. If there was a dimmer
switch in that bright season, she found it; learned you can
run wild as often as you like, but you must not faint.
If she bicycles into an afternoon foggy with mosquitoes,
mother-of-pearl for mourning, catch her, keep her and
keep her.

Hibernation

for Ginny

This morning begs for hibernation, the sinking that raindrops and grandchildren engender, all bleak and blurry around the edges—sound and not sound. I am ready to abandon myself to the duvet's promise of muffled comfort, the seduction of a few safer moments, but your postcard on my dresser stops me; that painting of autumn trees, like flames against a sky of lapis lazuli, laced through with amethyst: your art. You at eighty-one, announcing your latest show, make me sit to attention, reconsider the value of hibernation against the total hedonism of a sesame Ryvita just skimmed with butter, or what I don't know about socks—their mating habits, their death rituals, the lurk of new poems, and hibernation is postponed.

Migration

Blunt-kneed, and folded tight in V-formation
she hides from the day's disappointments like
a blind goose, leaves the clatter of morning
behind her, the flock's stragglers at a loss.
Here, thunder is muted, zag of lightning
dimmed by the fuggy down of her quilt. Grey-
tented she can find shelter from compulsion's
raw pull, can contemplate flight that ends
on milder shores where breathing may become
more viable, the heart's thump and rumble
more distant, where she can see the glimmer
of hope through the viscosity of angst,
take pleasure from small delights; the comfort
of the everyday; something like balance.

Compact

Sullen behind my cinnamon candle, December rain,
and I try to focus on the water table, its slow fill, its
subterranean mystery while old summers well up. Time
flips backward to anomalies of adoration: early offerings,
my first (and last) tennis racket, presented at birth to
guarantee no ball hit by me would ever clear the net.

For grazed knees, the comfort of iodine tincture, the sting,
the splodge of brown, a sign someone knew I was a child,
and I forgave again and again until the feisty bay mare
offered on my sixteenth; a gift that was never for me, a
terrifying treasure to give someone else an excuse to ride,
to persuade me horses were safe. After that, advice:

get squared away, get on the ball, sit the trot, seize the day,
don't let the bastards grind you down, nice girls don't...
so much wisdom for one young girl, but good grounding
for later: an impossible compact, when I never powdered,
tucked in a velvet bag, a peacock enamelled on the cover—
the wrong gift for the wrong woman at the wrong time;

from a man who should have known better. Drenched in
the aftermath of storm, a sunset of apricot and lavender, I wish
I could say I'd returned it, threw it in his face, against the wall,
in the bin, but the fact is, I use it still—am never without it, check
for flaws in its mirror: smeared mascara, tear damage, hairs that
sprout where they should not; the placement of tweezers.

Hold-all

Imagine a satchel large enough to contain
your grandmother's rocker (early American),
small enough to clasp your mother's ring—
star of sapphire—a gift on her sixteenth.

Imagine wrapping them up in your biggest fears;
along with the incense burners that never worked,
even though they came as gifts, came with love.
The empty packet that held their sticks

still smells wonderful, could envelop the rest
in beauty, next to the sound that's made
by chopping fresh coriander, its precise greenness,
keeping the back beat; drumming away

about climate change, held at bay by smells
of hot olive oil, fresh coffee, popcorn;
and on top, just room for that hard-bound copy
of *The Prophet*, by Kahlil Gibran.

Imagine the joy of the secret hiding place,
the padlock's reassuring rattle, in the one
spot that only you know about, underneath
your rib cage, just below your heart.

Mapping

for Jan

Over and over we are lost in some foreign place
that should be France but must be somewhere else
because we're climbing; climbing in a Gauloise fug,

the taste rank and raw, thinly covered with layers
of the chocolate you feed me, square by ragged square.
to keep me awake long enough, please God,

to get us somewhere before the lights fail again.
Behind us the engine is raucous, whining with the effort
of carrying us to where we may not want to go.

Around us are meadows of indigo and turquoise
like the ocean we crossed to find ourselves here,
still wrestling with confusion over men, love, mothers,

while the child we cart with us sits, Indian fashion,
on her door-to-door bed, eyes brimming with doubt
at our behaviour, at our folly, about the way we never quite

stop in time to buy milk, laugh too loudly, cough all night
like moribund consumptives and wake over and over
to find ourselves in the middle of places we should not be:

You remember the cowherd's path to milking,
how we were marooned with full bladders,
surrounded by hillocks of brown flanks, a sea of cows;

lumbering, their heads swaying, weighed down
with cathedral-size bells, their eyes, through coy lashes
full of friendly interest at our plight.

I remember the sound of other bells: a bicycle path
full of industrial-weight machines, angry rural commuters,
threatening us with raised fists, lunch-boxes, morning energy,

the way the brakes failed just outside Nancy, throwing us
at the mercy of a family of mechanics who ate and drank lunch
forever, course by sumptuous course, while we looked on, famished.

Over and over we tell ourselves we have arrived in safety
at where we should be, but the bewilderment of the journey
haunts us; we continue to career through unmapped land.

Sea Facing

In my first wild waking,
behind the curtains
the sea waits: a slice of light,
the rope-pulls, their tassels,
an explosion of dust disturbed,
the impossibility of sleep. Down
a corridor of sun to the cobbled shore
I remember how everything begins
with water: the womb dance,
the last safe swim, the first hint
of drowning, the amniotic rush
of morning.

Naked Man Shovelling Snow

Sierra Hot Springs

The naked man shovels snow
as if it was weightless as winter sky
pinked up for early sunset.
He flashes a hearty mountain smile

that says: hi, I'm okay; how about you?
His skinny plait swings to-and-fro in time
with his shrivelled scrotum, while his penis,
curls up tight to keep warm, like a rosebud
caught by October frost. I scrunch down

inside my borrowed swim suit, consider
how bodies can look so tough and tender
at once; how hard it gets to be proud of goose-
bumped flesh, age-creased skin; the way

the mountains don't give a damn; the polite steam
from the sulphur spring that fails to conceal.

Geography Lesson

I see you're missing from my map of the world—
not like Malta—
small, dark and spoiled,
or Barbados,
spicy and indigestible,
or even Britain,
rife with May blossom
and petrol fumes.

More like dog-faced Australia,
vast and multi-faceted,
or North America—
snow-capped on top,
azure and bone-dry below:
everything and nothing at once.

Like Gibraltar,
you're slipping away sideways,
and your absence
has been noted.

Going Without Saying

Tie your scarf under your chin, brisk and taut; hang your apron
on the hook above the stove, its mouth wide open and empty,

stained black with family fires, the handles of the pots torqued
into unlikely shapes. The stepping stones don't know

you've swept your last; that the moss has already sown its seeds. Just
walk away from the sad-eyed shutters, painted pink when you thought

you might stay on. Walk past the Sweet Williams, they'll only fade;
the Irises that shake their gaudy beards, leaf spikes fierce as swords

grouped at their feet. Don't look back at that window pane, splintered
when the first bombs fell, slivers raining down like crystal

on Baka's linen cloth, the silver hand-polished by Yelena, bought cheap
in that Belgrade shop; the symmetry of your evening shattered.

Leave the door open; there's nothing left to steal—just paint peeling
in brown flakes like dried blood. Turn your back on the arch

with its faded paper bows, mementos of your wedding day. Walk fast
past the photos of your recent dead, draped with floral tributes in plastic

to last forever. Slip between the stone lions, their gaze that gives
away nothing. Walk right away from the rub of sack cloth,

the sprinkle of ashes, creamy saucers of elderflower, edible mimosa.
Leave the wind to spread the news.

Fossils

How swimming naked in the Baltic, your
toes are lapped from nine shores
by sweet and salty waves.

How the reeds, blue-green and toxic
twist around your thighs
permissibly intimate,

and this far north the day goes on until
morning, every scrap of sunshine
up for grabs. How

Prussian Frederick orders amber in bulk
for his room, and you want to be
trapped there forever.

How afternoons are accordions and Chekhov
with air that's lingon blue, the taste
of tart green schnapps, and Olga

orders champagne which Anton hasn't drunk
for ages, and he says you don't put ice
on an empty heart and dies.

How the white-tailed eagle finds the right
tree at last, and a mate—
starts a nest.

The Man who was Excited by Poppies

Was it the enticement
of peering over the edge, deep
into the chasm of each blossom,
where he breathed-in possibility,
touched the musky magenta
that welcomed and alarmed him
but faded and fell in the space
of a day?

Or was it just the petals—that
Russian pink, sudden as rainbows,
with the fragrance of fungi
after showers, caviar on ice—the scent
of surrender that made him
take the plunge, again and
again, knowing he would
regret and regret it?

Epithalamium

The speed's a surprise; the way the roof
of the church disappears, licked by a line
of gingerbread glow that splits the pillar
behind her head while the edges curl in disdain.
The veil's a revelation, a canopy of sparks
like the tail of a comet that dwindles to a halo
round her face, grabs hair, eats eyebrows,
flattens nose, smears the smile of triumph, then
dives for the cleavage that made her mother
wince, crumples the tight waist, picks up
momentum on the train, wolfs down slippers
in a single greedy gulp. The groom melts more
slowly—an eternity of worsted, of waistcoat
and cravat, fizzles out, leaves a sticky film
that's washed down the plughole. Stainless
steel has no back draft, allows no ashes.

Instant Messaging

Weeks might pass
on the peak of a wave,
the creak of the rigging,
the navigator's rum moment.
In nights without a single star
a lover, a wife, a child,
might die,
so far away, they could
hang suspended
in the world of the living
for weeks, for months,
before the news arrived
bringing delayed tears,
funeral crepe.

There could be weeks,
even months, of lingering
at sea, of blissful illusion—
the uninformed imagination
taking delight in tame parrots
in the drollery of marmots—
tasting cassava or breadfruit,
the conversation idle, optimistic,
over pineapple, papaya, a tang
to challenge the breakfast palate,
before the letter, brown
with travel, arrived
delivered delayed tears,
funeral crepe.

Muntjac

Not your everyday pet, he grins, the young
stable-hand, shakes mud and grass from riding
boots, with the animal draped over his arm,
dangling stiff-legged, all points pointed: hooves,
dainty but sharp, needle nose softened by its doe-
still gaze, braced for tears. It's the gaze disturbs;
shapes what comes next; the waiting room hushed,
for each of us will drive tonight through dark lanes
where creatures wait to leap into our paths.
Together we lean in, urge him to jump the queue—
let the deer go first—and as the door shuts, breathe
out; tell tales of journeys that end in small deaths.

Rough Draft–Easter

Blossoms flare, a mist of pink,
white, grey, smoking out
winter. Leaves so tender

they've yet to learn green, well up
like tears. This month aches
with birth and death.

Hedge-row thorns tear at cloth,
at flesh. The fields are full of lambs
that know only the milky teat,

the fug of ewe's pelt, the beginnings
of a taste for blades of grass. And I
remember the child, faintly drawn

in a Michelangelo sketch, who tugs
at his father's sleeve, longs to escape
what must come next in the story—

the certainty of loss; the absence
of miracles.

And Only Today

As out of place as
chimney sweeps and just
as black—blink and you'll
miss them. One by one

the horses are unloaded,
a wary stepping down, their legs
slender as show girls', the carriage
a prop in their play; their heads,

regal with responsibility,
plumes nod, shiver. The drivers,
their supporting cast, incongruous
in top hats, take up whips,

reins, and they are off.
Three shiny limousines
follow, stately anachronisms,
as the full cortege slips past.

Time slows, stops.
The twig broom trees
of early winter sweep the sky,
brisk with authority.

Pennsylvania Prim

*...There will be no flowers, sung hymns, or mention of the lives they
touched in accordance with their belief that people should not be praised too
much; that all praise goes to God...*

Fox News, 9/10/2006

This poem wants to bolt, tugs at the reins,
tosses its head
shakes itself like a nervous filly

but shies away from words
for that October morning,
for the cornfield husked and frosted.

From behind its creamy clapboard
the schoolhouse looks out—
simplicity in life and also in death.

where the boys, set free, hunkered down
with mothers and babies
prayed and cried their fear. Ten

Amish schoolgirls lined up against
the blackboard, white-capped,
compliant, Pennsylvania prim,

gunned down by a milkman, just
finished his rounds. Thirty-four
horse-drawn buggies pull up hard

to hilltop graves, five carry plain pine
coffins—*an Amish female
is laid to rest in a white cap and dress,*

and there will be no mention of their smiles
the lives they touched;
nor will there be singing. Words will fail.

77

Piroshka

My hand edges towards the cuff
through the cave of the sleeve
where the fur embraces my arm.

A ripe rush of new leather rises
around me as I pull the matching toque
over my forehead. My cheekbones

push up high under my Kirghiz eyes
as I fasten the braided loops over the toggles
tight across my breasts, my heart—feel

fur-lined boots creep over my ankles
up my calves while Vronsky watches
from the troika. There is the cry

of Siberian wolves, but I ignore
their portent, though the horses stamp
and steam, their hooves nervous.

My head is full of samovars, pale tea
in tall glasses with filigree holders that sear
my fingers—the transparency of lemon slices.

My feet are running, slipping on frozen
snow, as my voice calls out in another
language that might be Russian, and I feel
the steam of a screaming train.

Vladimirka Road

...after Levitan and Akhmatova

Here, with the ache of the miles ahead,
I search the ground for the print
of your heels, wonder—were you bootless,
barefoot, bleeding by now—if I've left it
too late. But the driver will take me no further—
the horse, grey-muzzled, wants feeding,
rubbing down. From here I must make my way
alone. My boots, God willing, are stout enough.
Ahead is flat and green, fields that stretch
to tall blue forest where the world

comes to an end. *What is flat to the eye*
may not be so to the feet, I hear you say,
hear you laugh, and rusty-voiced, I thank
the driver, wonder when I will speak
to another human soul, to you (are you alive?)
to your wardens (are they, God willing, kind?)
Dos vidanya, says the driver, nods, grins,
gap-toothed. Crack of whip, clatter of wheels—
I'm alone. Ahead is a shrine to their virgin,

not mine, but still I am drawn to it, my feet lift
unbidden, stumble on this road that is barely
a road. I have had little use for prayer,
but there are messages to leave, a tale to be
collected by someone, of where I have been,
where I must go. I pull my shawl around me,
tight against the mutinous wind, shoulder
my cloth bag, feel the shift and crunch
of day-old bread; the reassurance of water jugs
rubbing against one another inside it.

Shifting

Seeing herself in hotel mirrors,
corners are turned:
not smoothly,
the gears shifting without effort,
and brakes barely discernible, but
stark and abrupt—the wheels
churn up loose gravel,
hurl it against the windscreen.

And the squeal of tyres under stress
is her own anguished voice,
protesting the race with time.

UNIVERSITY OF WINCHESTER
LIBRARY